INTERVAL AND MAJOR SCALE THEORY

THEORY

Bryan DeLauney

ISBN: 0615966985
ISBN-13: 978-0615966984

A special thanks to http://jguitar.com/ for allowing me to use their scale diagrams and chord charts!!
Go visit their site, its great!.

CONTENTS

Contents

ACKNOWLEDGMENTS

I'd like to thank all of the people that have helped me along the way and those who have believed in me. Thanks to my dear and lovely wife for all of her support. Thanks above all to my Lord and Savior, Jesus Christ!

Chapter 1 – *Introduction*

Music is a never ending cycle of heartbreak and happiness.

I have spent many years learning how to play the guitar. I spent countless hours running scales and memorizing things, until I started feeling pretty good about myself. Then I go to YouTube and see a 12 year old prodigy practically annihilate all of my success in one long arpeggio that I could never play if I had seventeen fingers and 3 hands.

That's the breaks in music. There are these mini-Mozarts that are born with the innate ability to make all in their path feel inferior. Most of us have to work really hard at it and get lost a lot along the way. I know that there were many times that I felt defeated.

I started taking guitar lessons when I was 15 years old. When I initially took lessons, my teacher gave me a lesson that had all of the modes on it and he wanted me to learn them. The only problem is that after I spent 30 seconds memorizing the finger patterns (I started playing guitar at 12), I still knew nothing. He never explained it to me, and that is way more intricate than I needed to know at week one to begin with.

I hadn't been educated at all in any theory and modes is a bit up the tree for me at that time. All things need a starting point. All education needs to be grounded in reality. You have to start at the beginning and then build up to where you want to be. I didn't go that route. I spent many years not having a clue what I was playing, like most guitar players.

I decided that once and for all that I wanted to know what I was doing. I wanted to be able to communicate with musicians. I didn't want to be classified as a mere guitar player. A guitar player, to most other instrument players, is the barbarian class in most role playing type of games. They walk in, bash the crap out of everything in sight, get all the credit, yet have no idea what they did, nor how they did it.

I didn't want to be like that. I wanted to be like the great sage that everyone comes to for answers. I wanted to play stuff that sounded good, but didn't make sense to the untrained and musically ignorant. No, a guitar player wasn't what I wanted to be. I wanted to be a musician.

In order to get there I taught myself. Was that the best way to do it? Probably not, but it was all that I had at the time. The way that I did it was to sit at a table, with a pencil and paper, and write stuff down until I figured it out. I read stuff here and there, but it didn't make much sense to the musically dumb and staff notation ignorant. I wrote down major scales and chords and everything I could think of, looking for relationships and answers.

I was in a bit of a loss until one day I was at work and this guy that drove a fork lift happened to have a degree in music had a conversation with me. The thing that set it all off for me was when he said that it's all in how it relates to the C major scale. That was the bit of knowledge that I needed to grow from and I figured it out from there.

My books that I write are not a fanciful way to regurgitate the same old garbage that you couldn't understand before. I am writing about how I learned this with a pencil and a sheet of paper. This is how I memorized things and looked at them from a human perspective. This is the real deal when it comes to theory and how to understand it. I have read through college music theory text books and they contain the same information that I present to you; just in a real language that you can understand.

This book isn't about trying to look brilliant. I am not trying to impress the musical intellect that have their proverbial noses in the air, snubbing all of us peasantly unlearned. I want the regular Joe/Josina, who sits on his/her bed and wants to learn how to really play music, and understand it. I will write just like I am now to you, and I will write something stupid to help you learn it, or say something completely corny so that you won't be so bored and want to give up, and I will hopefully teach you something about music.

Here is the rest of the speech:

Theory takes away the guesswork in music. Why do some scales sound good over certain chords and others don't? What scale can I play over a certain chord progression? What is a key? How do I know what chords to use? What in the world is a Cmin7b5? What is the difference between major and minor? These can all be answered in this book, plus many other questions.

There is too much information in music for one to just store it in virtual memory. When there are so many different scales and modes, it helps to refer back to a piece of paper to visualize things. The vision helps to lock things into memory and writing things down is also a memory tool. Use a pen and paper…. For real. No joke.

Now let's talk about music. I do understand that most people will brush over the introduction like it is a waste of time, and get on with the cool stuff, but just give me a minute to get the ball rolling. Use this book as a reference, guide, tool, kindling, torch, I don't care really. But, if you want to get something out of music you need to know that music is not how many notes you can play a second, it's not how cool you are, it isn't how smart you are, nor is it how many scales you can memorize.

Music is in the mind, it is a rhythm, a melody. All of the scales in the world will make you a better nobody, but using one scale wisely will make you a star. Practice. Study. When you start a new section, understand it fully before you move on. When you play a new scale or mode, don't just memorize it and move to the next one. Put on a jam track and try to use it. Integrate it into your playing and go from one scale that you know into the new scale you just learned. Do that before you move on and it will come together more smoothly.

Claude Debussy said wisely, "Music is the space between the notes". I happen to agree with that statement. Don't get me wrong, I can hang with the best of them, but there is more to music than fast, long runs. Try to embellish notes with overly dramatic bends, slides, reverse bends, vibrato, and timing. Every note doesn't have to be 1/16 or 1/8. Try holding notes for longer periods than you would normally and see how they sound. Record your practices and listen to them. Hear your mistakes before others do.

I am not going to teach you what a bend is or how to tune your guitar. This book is about theory and how to use your brain. I don't intend on writing tons of "licks", but I do intend to educate you on how to overcome the stumbling block of knowledge. I want you to come away from this understanding theory and not be afraid of it. I have heard a million guitarists say that theory wasn't important, yet they didn't know the difference between an A minor and a coal miner.

Don't be a chump musician. Lay off the A and E minor pentatonic scales. In fact, forget about them, entirely if you could. I apologize about that, ok no I don't. I don't like the pentatonic scale, yet I will teach on it, but every bozo in the world plays that and 99% of them sound exactly alike. If you can play them like say, Dave Sabo from Skid Row that would be awesome. If you play them like, I don't know say, your neighbor, stop now.

This book is not intended to be a standalone, learn it all, and know everything kind of book. There is so much involved in music theory that people get doctorates in the subject. There is no way I can cover that level in one book. This book should coincide either with prior knowledge and/or lessons. The fundamentals of theory are not difficult. They aren't exceptionally easy, nor are they insanely unlearnable. Take your time. You don't have to read this book in a day. Take small bites, work hard, study, use your pen and paper, ask your instructor or someone who knows (email a music professor) if you have questions, and enjoy yourself. You play a guitar not work a guitar. Make it fun.

Ok. I get the question on if I have the knowledge, how do I apply it. The key to knowledge is understanding. Having knowledge is useless unless you understand the knowledge you possess. I have decided to insert a section at the end of every chapter on how to use what has been learned from that chapter. It won't be exhaustive, but may give you an idea on why you just worked so hard.

Take the time to see the relationships between scales, keys, chords, etc. How do these chords relate? How do these three chords in this chord pattern relate to the notes in the scale playing over them? The take home lesson here is relationships. Look at the notes. Compare notes in chords. Compare notes in scales. Compare notes from scales to chords.

Let's get started learning!!!

Chapter 2 - *Intervals Intro*

In order to first learn about theory, we must understand how to talk theory. In order to talk theory, we must know the vocabulary. In order to know the vocabulary, we must know the alphabet. Have I bored you yet?

Intervals are the basic building block in music. Intervals help us communicate to one another in a music language. Intervals allow us to build scales, chords, phrases, etc. An interval is the "distance" between pitches. Merriam-Webster defines it as "difference in pitch between tones". But there is more to an interval than the difference in pitch, and yet, there isn't. Don't let me confuse you by saying this. Let me show you…

Let's look at the notes in music. I always ask a student, "How many notes are on your guitar" and they look at me like I'm asking them to do some of that "new math". I then surprise them when I answer, 12. There are only twelve notes. In Western music and I don't mean Country and Western music, there are only 12 notes.

In Western music (further to be referred to as music) the smallest movement is called a semitone. This would be the equivalent of playing one of your guitar strings open, then fretting it on the first fret, or going from the first fret to the second. I think you get the picture. That's the smallest movement you can make.

The notes that we use are thus:

Table 2-1:

$$ A - A\# - B - C - C\# - D - D\# - E - F - F\# - G - G\# $$

Then it starts back over at *A* (The solitary note "A" is confusing, so I will make it bold when I am talking about a note). Table 2-1 is commonly referred to as the chromatic scale. Chroma means color in Greek, so apparently this is the colorful scale; a bit boring to me, but nevertheless, the chromatic scale.

All of your music learning will be based on this scale. You should know it. You should memorize it. Just remember that all notes *A – G* have a sharp (**#**) except the *E* and the *B*, so no sharp *ElB*ows. I hope that was dumb enough to retain in your memory; do a note-to-self on this idea (whenever you see **_NTS_** that means note-to-self, or it would be a good idea to remember this). If you notice that there are no flat (***b***) notes. That is because there are two, count em', two chromatic scales. Actually there is only one, but a second has what is called enharmonic notes.

Enharmonic notes are where one note has two different names. The reason this is done is to make it less confusing (not to you right now) and so that sheet music is less messy.

Less confusing? Well, it's like this… When you are writing a scale, using some of the modern steps (later in theory) you could end up with a *C* going to a *C#*. This would be confusing going from a *C* to a *C#*. The next step after the *C#* would more than likely be an *E*. Trust me, I've driven this car before. It would make much more sense to go from a *C* to a *Db* then to an *E*. Doesn't that look better than *C-C#-E*?

When connecting notes together in a scale it is normal to write it with dashes (-) in between the notes, i.e., *A-B-C-D-E-F-G*, just like we did in Table 2-1.

So, enharmonic notes are two notes that look differently, but mean the same thing, e.g. *A#* and *Bb*. If you are interested, and you should be, then you have another way of looking at the twelve notes:

Table 2-2:

A – Bb – B – C – Db – D – Eb – E – F – Gb – G – Ab

Then it starts over again at *A*.

Let's go over this, for the ones who need a little help. The # means sharp and the *b* means flat. When you move up, i.e. from the first fret to the second fret, you sharpen the pitch. When you move down, i.e. from the second fret to the first fret, you flatten the pitch. With this said, if you start on the 5th string (the second string from the top) or *A*-string open (not fretted) the pitch is an *A*. If you move up the guitar (linearly, on one string) every fret you move up will sharpen and it will correspond with Table 2-1 and Table 2-2 (see Figure 2-1, notice that the pattern starts over at 12).

Figure 2-1.

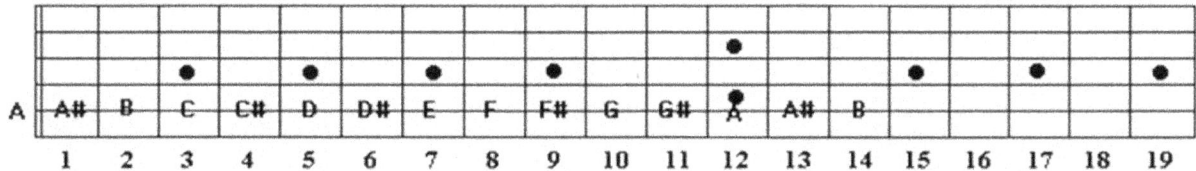

Notice that the A string is on the second from the bottom line. This drawing has the perception that you are laying the guitar down in your lap and viewing it from above. TAB uses the same principle.

The notes *A B C D E F G* are called naturals. The in-between notes *A# C# D# F# G#* or enharmonically, *Bb Db Eb Gb Ab* are called accidentals (**NTS**). These will be used for the rest of your life, if you don't give up music that is, and if you did, shame on you. I can't bold enough the NTS for you to know the chromatic scale, in both sharps and flats so don't let me down.

Now, these notes, when put into the context of a scale, are called intervals.

RECAP:

♫ There are 12 notes in Western music.

♫ The smallest movement between notes is a semitone.

♫ All semitones linked together is called the chromatic scale.

♫ There are 2 chromatic scales, one using sharps and one using flats.

♫ These are the same scales using enharmonic notes.

♫ Use your melon and memorize the chromatic scale!

Chapter 3 - *Intervals in Depth*

I hope that the last chapter went well. If not, take a few moments to look over it again. It's about to get more complicated, not in a bad way though. Take a deep breath, throw coffee in your face… let's go!

The intervals on sheet music look like this:

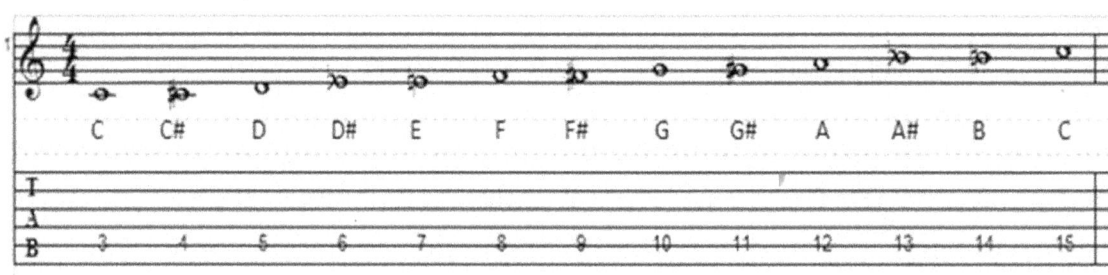

Figure 3-1.

The program that I am using to TAB and notate the music automatically generates the sharps and flats based on its internal programming corresponding to the key signature, so don't pay too much mind to that, right now. The point is you can see what it looks like. See the *C* to *C#* and then the *D* to *D#*? In this program it went from *D* to *Eb*. You can tell because it is on a different line. That is the less confusing part again, from the last chapter. In notation, enharmonic notes reduce the amount of sharp and flat signs and spaces the notes out, so you can read them easier.

When you play notes one after the other, it is called a melodic interval. If you played notes at the same time it's called a harmonic interval. If you play a solo you build a melody, but if you play a chord the notes need to harmonize (consonance, sound good together) or it sounds like junk (dissonance).

An interval can be associated by a quality and a number. The number is the easy part; the quality may take a little memorizing. Let me list the qualities, first.

Perfect, Major, minor, Augmented, and *diminished*

There are two terms to know when talking about these, consonance and dissonance. Consonance means that it sounds good together or has stability. Dissonance, on the other hand, means that it doesn't sound so good, sounds terrible, or is unstable. This can be viewed as notes that when played together or when in relation to one another are pleasing to listen to or you want to break the dude's guitar over his face.

Perfect intervals are considered perfectly consonant. The major, minor, augmented, and diminished are considered to be less consonant than the Perfect intervals.

The augmented interval means that it is a semitone bigger than the interval "should" be, i.e., a perfect fourth raised a semitone becomes an augmented fourth. Augmented means "increased" or "made larger" in Latin.

Diminished means "decreased" or "made smaller" in Latin, so this is an interval that is made smaller, i.e., a perfect fifth lowered by a semitone becomes a diminished fifth.

Perfect consonance – Unison and Octave, Perfect 4th and Perfect 5th.

Imperfect consonance – Major 3rd and minor 6th, minor 3rd and Major 6th.

Dissonant intervals – minor 2nd and Major 7th, Augmented 4th and diminished 5th

This may not make sense at the moment. Just remember that we are building something. It will come together in the end.

Let's say you are tuning your guitar and you play the top string, 5th fret (*A*). Then you strike the second to the top string open, at the same time. If the guitar is in tune, you will hear *Perfect consonance*, or unison. If the open string, *A* is out of tune, then you will hear a wobbling sound, called *dissonance*, until the note goes in tune with the other.

What's happening here is that the sound wave, when in consonance, is riding along nicely with the other wave. When a sound wave from one note adds, subtracts, or interferes with another sound wave, you can hear it. Humans generally hear the pleasantness of certain corresponding frequencies and dislike waves that crash or greatly disturb other sound waves.

There's a term, roughness, which refers to that wobbling sound you hear when tuning a guitar. The wobbles, called beat tones (Fig 3-2), are either pleasing to the ear, or torturous.

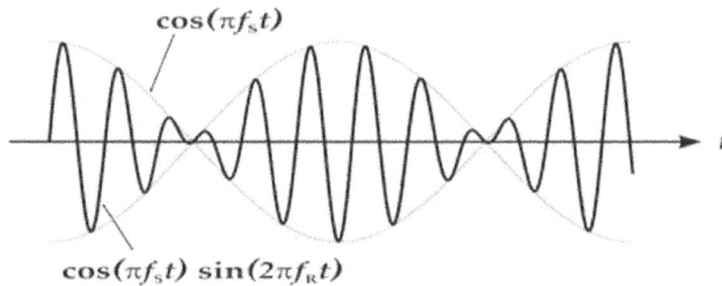
Some people spent time figuring out what most of us know by listening and graphed out the roughness for us (Fig 3-3). The most harmonic of tones end up giving us the diatonic scale, an eight note musical scale that has seven tones and an octave.

Figure 3-3.

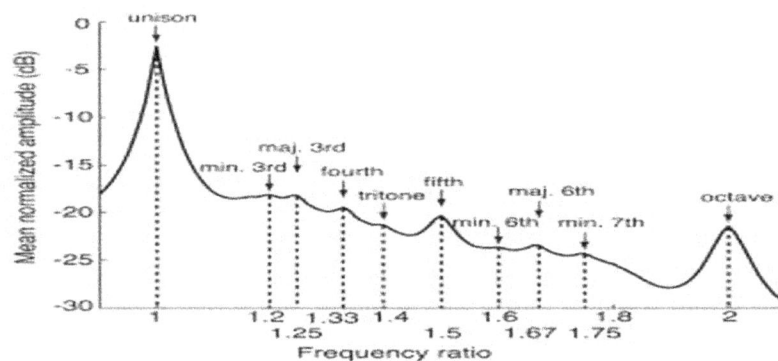

Roughness graph

The take home message is that there is a reason we use certain frequencies for intervals and there are reasons why we pick out certain intervals to make the diatonic scale, which will be the foundation to all of your music theory. We also now somewhat know what consonance and dissonance are and that some notes in the diatonic scale are more consonant or dissonant than others. These consonant or dissonant notes are either called perfect, major, minor, augmented, or diminished.

Figure 3-4

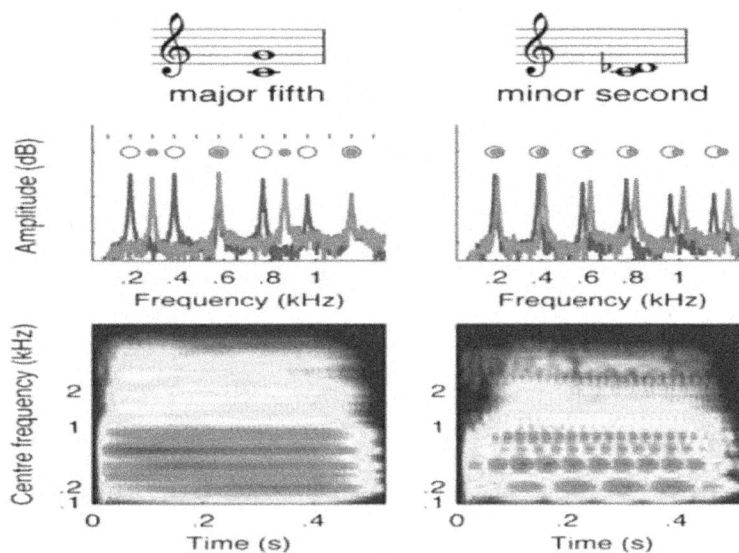

Difference in roughness and beat tone of m2 vs. P5 intervals.

Figure 3-4 shows a clear example of consonance and dissonance. On the left, you can see the perfect 5th and on the right is the minor second. The minors second, being one semitone away from the root note is virtually the same note, but not quite. Thinking about it as if it were a wave, you'd have a wave going out and then another which it peaks a split second after the original note (because its frequency is a little different) and the waves hit each other and cause a disturbance.

This beating (beat tone) in the minor 2nd (red) and the original root tone (blue) can be seen in Fig. 3-4. The beating is more evident in the bottom right picture of Fig. 3-4. The upper right image shows how the waves don't coincide together.

The perfect 5th, displayed in Fig. 3-4, has its red peaks either in the middle of the root tone (blue) peaks, or they peak together, when both notes are struck and held. If you look at the graph, moving right is a held note's waves cycling over a period of time. So, the perfect 5th waves and the root note waves don't interfere with one another. Looking at the bottom left image of Fig. 3-4, you don't see the beating like in the m2 interval.

We now need to make sense of the waves as it compares to the guitar. The guitar string is the wave generator. When you strike it with your plectrum (pick) a wave is created from the oscillation of the string. The oscillation is based on the tension and the length of the string. Notice that no matter how hard you strike the string, it doesn't change the pitch of the note produced.

I want to make this more apparent by using the analogy of a rubber band. Everyone has put a rubber band between their first finger and their thumb and struck it, with the other hand, to make a sound. If you haven't done this, you have lived a sad and boring existence.

If you pinch the rubber band between your thumb and forefinger where it hangs limp, with no tension, and pluck it with the other hand then not only does it not make a sound, but you probably look like a chimp staring at a computer. Because it has no tension in it, no oscillation can occur, thus not generating a sound wave.

When you have your thumb and forefinger extended and the rubber band around them, the further you pull your finger and thumb apart, the higher the pitch of the rubber band. If you shortened the rubber band, by tying a knot in it, then there would be more tension in the string at the same width as before and the pitch would be higher than it was without the knot.

On a guitar, the concept is the same. The string is held at a static distance when open. It is the length from the bridge to the nut. When tuning a string, and you tighten the string with the tuning pegs, you add tension to the string, increasing its pitch. If you loosen the string with the tuning pegs, the pitch gets lower.

When you fret a guitar, you shorten the string which increases the pitch. This can be explained in mathematical terms with the following equation $v = f * \lambda$ [The speed (v) is equal to the frequency (f) multiplied by the wave length (λ)]. In this case the speed is the speed of sound, which is 343 meters per second (m/s).

Figure 3-5:

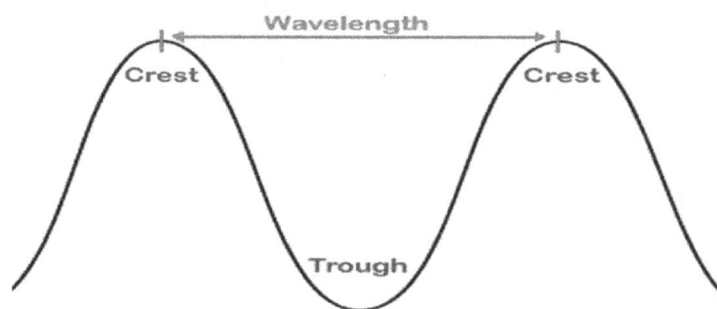

An open *A* is at a frequency of 440 hertz (Hz), and Hz means cycles per second.

Figure 3-5 shows us that a wavelength is just as it sounds. It is the length of one wave. If we go back to our equation and insert the known values we get $343\frac{m}{s} = 440\,Hz * \lambda$

We then use some simple algebra and get $\frac{343\frac{m}{s}}{440\,cycles/s} = \lambda$. We do the math and get 0.78 meters. What if the wavelength was halved to 0.39 meters? We would get the equation $\frac{343\,m/s}{0.39\,meters} = f$. Do the division and we get 880 ‾s or 880 cycles/sec or 880 Hz. That means when we half the wavelength, we double the frequency, which is an octave.

This is considered some magic, naturally occurring anomaly, that the doubled frequency is equivalent to an octave. An Octave is $f*2^n$ the frequency of a note (n is an integer). Therefore, $220*2^1 = 440$; $220*2^2 = 880$; $110*2^3 = 880$; $110*2^4 = 1760$ (all in Hz).

All this means is 110 Hz, 220 Hz, 440 Hz, 880 Hz, and 1760 Hz are all *A*s.

I hope that you have learned what is going on with the notes and pitches as we progress down the fretboard. When playing a guitar, the waves are produced based on how we manipulate the oscillation of the strings. These waves interact with other waves in either a constructive or destructive way. The way that these waves interact cause consonance or dissonance.

Let's complete our discussion on the perfect, minor, major, augmented, and diminished qualities.

I know that guitarists use TAB, and I will refer to stuff, when possible in TAB, but music theory and staff notation coincide, because staff is a visual representation of the theory that is occurring. I'll explain right now.

We'll learn about the qualities and we'll see them as they relate in the staff notation. Let's refresh and move on –

Perfect, *Major*, *minor*, *Augmented*, and *diminished*

These are the qualities of the intervals. Remember there are qualities and numbers when referring to intervals. I said the numbers were easy and I am about to tell you why.

The numbers refer to their staff position (Figure 3-6). You have to count the lines and the spaces. It moves from the bottom toward the top; the bass notes are low on the staff and they get higher in pitch as you move up the staff. If there was a note on the bottom line and a note on the second from the bottom line, they would be a 3rd apart. **NTS**, you count the initial note.

Figure 3-6

Staff position

Figure 3-7

P1 m2 M2 m3 M3 P4 A4 P5 m6 M6 m7 M7 P8

Figure 3-7 shows the quality, the number, and the staff notation. Notice, there are only 8 numbers? You were supposed to remember these:

A – A# – B – C – C# – D – D# – E – F – F# – G – G#

A – Bb – B – C – Db – D – Eb – E – F – Gb – G – Ab

Notice that there are only 7 letters, *A-B-C-D-E-F-G?*

Each line represents a note letter. The sharp or flat is added to the note to distinguish its character (**NTS**). This isn't a book on staff, but some will have to be learned to be able to understand what's going on, understand the visual representations, and for the future of you musical travels. You don't necessarily need to be able to sight read to know what we are talking about.

There are 3 fundamental symbols in musical notation the sharp *(#)*, flat *(b)*, and the natural *(♮)*. These change the natural, written on the staff, to an accidental (not the ♮. It tells you to go back from an accidental to a natural, as you further read that note in this one measure.) . Example 3-1 shows how a C is sharpened to a C# and then comes back to a natural C. Also note that when the C is naturalized again, it doesn't carry any sign (the last note). It works the same way if it was sharpened or flattened. Once it changes in that measure, it is considered changed until the next measure.

Example 3-1:

Example 3-2 shows how a sharpened note in staff carries the changed value until the next measure. In the second measure, the C# is indicated in the first note of the measure, but not the following, until the note is played again in the following measure. Then it is naturalized again in the third measure of Example 3-2.

Example 3-2:

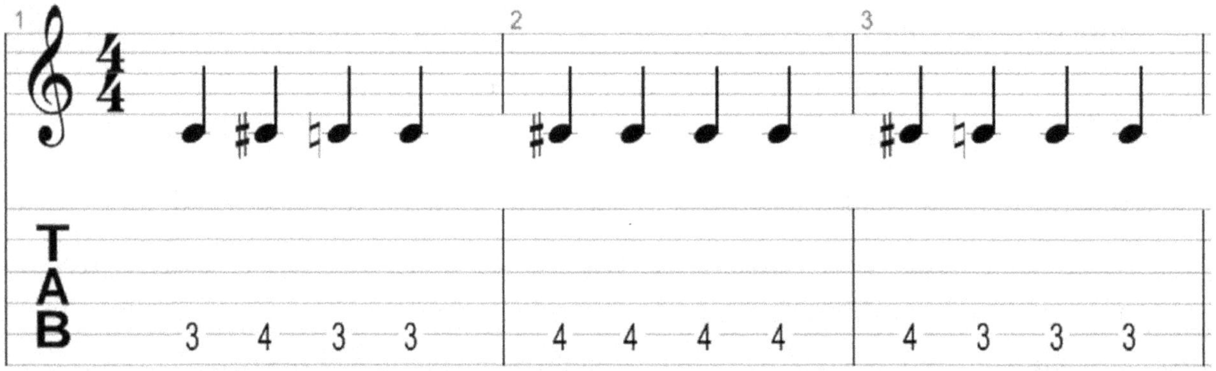
T
A
B
3 4 3 3
4 4 4 4
4 3 3 3

There are 7 naturals and 5 accidentals totaling 12 notes, and thus; we have 12 intervals. The P8 is the same as the 1st note at a higher register, but a ***C*** is a ***C*** is a ***C***, and we refer to it as starting over at 1.

Figure 3-6:

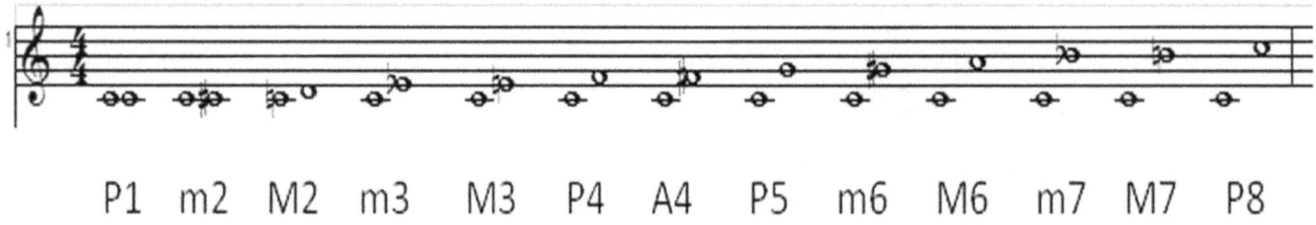
P1 m2 M2 m3 M3 P4 A4 P5 m6 M6 m7 M7 P8

I reintroduced Figure 3-6 from the other page so we can see with our new found knowledge the difference between these intervals.

[P1] – It's essentially the same note.

m2 – One semitone away from the root note.

[M2] – One tone (2 semitones) from the root note.

m3 – Three semitones from the root note. This is a minor third.

[M3] – Two whole tones (4 semitones) from the root note. A major third.

[P4] – Five semitones from the root note.

A4 – Three whole tones aka the tritone (6 semitones) from the root note.

[P5] – Seven semitones from the root note.

m6 – Four whole tones (8 semitones) from the root note.

[M6] – Nine semitones from the root note.

m7 – Five whole tones (10 semitones) from the root note.

[M7] – Eleven semitones from the root note.

[P8] – The same note as the root, but at double the frequency, e.g. 440 Hz to 880 Hz. This is also called the octave, root, tonic, and sometimes written 8va.

How to use this:

C-D-E-F-G-A-B-C (**C** major Scale)

From the root note **C** to **D** is a Major second (M2), but a **C** to a **Db** is a minor second (m2). **C** to **E** is a Major 3ʳᵈ (M3) and a minor third (m3) would be **C** to **Eb**. **C** to **F** is a Perfect fourth (P4), but **C** to **F#** would be an Augmented fourth (A4). The **C** to **G** is a Perfect fifth, and the Augmented fifth would be the **C** to **G#**. If the scale already contained a P4, then there wouldn't be an A4. It would then be a diminished fifth (d5). This may sound confusing, but just like we needed all letters of the musical alphabet to make a diatonic scale, we also need each number. From **C** to **A** is Major sixth (M6), but you guessed it, a **C** to **Ab** is a minor sixth (m6). **C** to **B** is a Major seventh (M7), but **C** to **Bb** is a minor seventh (m7). **C** to **C** is a P8 or octave.

If you notice the brackets on the intervals in the list above; those are the intervals in the major scale (NTS). The other intervals are not in the major scale, that is not to say that they don't exist within diatonic scales (modes of the major scale, more specifically).

We can see that we have intervals that are either major or minor. If it isn't a perfect interval than the larger interval is the major and the smaller is the minor interval. The augmented or diminished are either a semitone greater or less than a perfect quality, but still has the same number of it.

These qualities and numbers are going to be a large part of your understanding and education of music. Knowing these and applying them will help tremendously, for instance, a melodic minor is the same as the major scale except it has a m3 instead of a M3 (Melodic minor is *C-D-Eb-F-G-A-B-C* where the *C* major scale is *C-D-E-F-G-A-B-C*. This is called the ascending melodic minor, but the descending melodic minor is actually the natural minor, confusing.. I know!)

RECAP:

♫ Notes played one after the other are melodic, played at the same time are harmonic.

♫ Consonance sounds good, dissonance sounds wobbly or bad.

♫ Intervals are named by quality and number

♫ Qualities are perfect, minor, major, augmented, and diminished.

♫ The interval numbers relate to the distance from the root in the staff notation.

♫ Intervals are frequencies that have the least roughness.

♫ In staff the lines and spaces get counted.

♫ There are only 7 intervals, because there are only 7 naturals.

♫ Accidentals are on the same line as the naturals, but are given sharp or flat signs to identify them.

♫ The octave is the root note generated at double the frequency, i.e., root is 440 Hz, the octave is 880 Hz.

♫ The octave is considered another root note and counted again as 1, not 8.

Chapter 4 - *Major Scale Theory Intro*

Picking up where we left off in the last chapter… We have the intervals, the qualities, and the numbers. We understand enough notation to be dangerous, and we're ready to put it into practice. So, let's take that knowledge you worked so hard for and combine it into something useful. Remember every house has a foundation, every tree has roots, and music's rooting foundation is intervals.

We are now moving from the chromatic scale into a useful scale and a scale that will determine the rest of 99% of any theory you will ever do; major scale theory. You must understand this to understand the rest of music. The relationship of adding and subtracting is to mathematics, as major scale theory is to music. Without adding and subtracting you have no multiplying, dividing, algebra, calculus, engineering, science, and even music uses it. The major scale is that important. I think so anyway…

In order to first go through the concepts, we need to know about steps. Steps are what we take to get somewhere, just like when we walk. We put one step in front of the other. In music we do the same thing. If you look at your guitar, or Diagram 4-1, you see strings and frets. Ignore the various strings and concentrate on the top string. Are you with me? Ok.

Diagram 4-1:

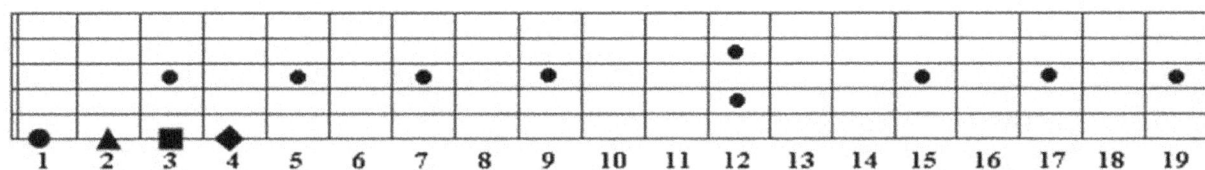

If we go linearly (up the neck from the nut toward the bridge) we traverse over frets. If we go from the 1st fret to the 2nd fret we have gone a half step (1/2 step or just H). If we go from the 1st fret to the 3rd fret then we have traveled a whole step (1 step or just W). Now if we go from the 1st fret to the 4th fret we have just made a one and a half step (1 ½ step).

How does this relate to intervals, you say? Intervals relate to the notes themselves (as they relate to another note) and scale steps refer to the space between consecutive notes. Remember the chromatic scale? It has a series of 12 semitones. So, moving from *C-C#* is a semitone; this is also called a half step. Therefore, a tone or whole step is *C-D*.

Look at it like this – you are at mile marker 1 and you go to mile marker 2, the distance is a mile. You aren't at a mile; you are at mile marker 2. You didn't travel a mile marker 2; you traveled a mile. As it refers to music – you play a perfect 5th, not a whole step. You moved a whole step, not a perfect 5th. The definition of a perfect 5th is a fifth spanning 7 semitones. You can play a perfect 5th but it has to be in relationship to something. Just like if you were running and you said that you ran a mile, not that you ran 5,280 feet, or 63,360 inches. An interval can be a composite distance whereas, a step is a solitary distance between consecutive notes. The m2 is one semitone from the root, C, but D# to E is a half step regardless of what the root note is (understand the difference?).

Table 4-1:

C	C#	D	D#	E	F	F#	G	G#	A	A#	B	C
Root	m2	M2	m3	M3	P4	A4	P5	A5	M6	m7	M7	Octave

Table 4-1 aligns the intervals with the notes starting with *C*. The *C major* scale will be the foundational major scale. You will see why, soon enough. **NTS** the P1 is also called the root or tonic, and the P8 is usually referred to as the octave (8va) or it is referred to as the root (because the scale continues again, my friend).

A major scale is built out of 8 intervals and 7 steps. In Table 4-2 below, the interval is associated with the note. The steps can be seen between them. In the C major scale, the C is the 1st interval, the D is the 2nd interval, the E is the 3rd interval, and so on and so forth. Notice that all notes have a sequential number (**NTS**). The root and the octave would be P1 and P8, respectively, but I want you to get used to seeing them as they are generally written, in practice.

Table 4-2.

Root		M2		M3		P4		P5		M6		M7		8va
	W		*W*		*H*		*W*		*W*		*W*		*H*	
C		D		E		F		G		A		B		C

Also take a note in Table 4-2 we use one scale alphabet letter for each interval. There is no letter skipping in the major scale. That is why we use enharmonic notes. By flattening notes or sharpening them we end up with all different notes. This will be more obvious later, but make a **NTS** of it.

How is this important?

This is the language of love, man! This is music talk. Go to some websites that actually talk about music and not some horse hockey, play guitar in 4 hours without trying site. You will see this terminology and see that minor scales, chords, arpeggios, modes, and etc., are derived from steps, intervals, and the foundational major scale.

Regarding the interval qualities, we can have various types of intervals because as you can see from Table 4-1 there are twelve notes and from the *C major* scale; above, there are only seven. That means there are 5 notes not being played. If you substitute / interchange a note then you have altered the scale and thus, the interval. Let me give you an example. If you have the *C major* scale (*C-D-E-F-G-A-B-C*) and you changed out the *D* for a *Db* (*C#*), then it isn't a *C major* scale anymore because the Major 2nd has been changed to a minor 2nd.

Alright, remember we have a Major (M), minor (m), Perfect (P), Augmented (A), and diminished (d). Seconds, thirds, sixths, and sevenths can all be *major* **or** *minor* intervals, but fourths, fifths, and octaves are called *perfect* intervals, in both major and minor keys.

Ok, if you didn't figure this out, the m2 is *minor* 2nd, the M2 is *major* 2nd, the P4 is *perfect* 4th, and the A4 is an *augmented* 4th. You can do the rest on your own. I have confidence in you.

Remember, the *C* major scale is *C-D-E-F-G-A-B-C and* we inserted a *Db* (*C #,* think enharmonic) in the place of a *D*. Notice that the interchanged note of *Db* (*C#* is the same thing,) for **D** takes the interval from a M2 to m2. You don't need to understand this fully, just the concept, right now.

Just remember that an interval is the distance from the 1st note (also called the root or tonic) to the next note. So, the 2nd interval is the 2nd note in the scale, and it will correspond with either a m2 or a M2 depending on the distance between the 1st note and the 2nd. For example, say I am playing in the key of *C* major, the *C* is the 1st note and the next note I play is a **D**. The **D** is the 2nd interval in the scale. You can see in Table 4-1 that **D** is the M2 (Major 2nd) compared to the root (*C*). Also, remember from the last chapter that the M2 is one whole tone (two semitones) from the root note.

Using this terminology one could say that they were playing off of the 3rd of the chord. This would mean that they would be playing a scale as it relates to the chord in general, but more specifically how it relates to the 3rd note in the chord. This goes into chord theory, but you get the idea that the terminology is important to know before you move on. One could also say that they were playing a minor third in the place of where a major third of a scale is supposed to be played (consequently making a melodic minor, as seen on page 18).

When playing *C* major:

C – the first note, P1, tonic, or root note.

D – the second note or M2.

E – the third or M3.

F – the fourth of the scale or P4.

G – the fifth or P5

A – the sixth in the *C* major scale or M6.

B – the seventh or M7.

C – The P8, or octave, 8va, root, tonic, etc.

From – To	Interval	Full Interval Name	Sound
C – C	P1	Perfect Unison	Perfect Consonance
C – D	M2	Major Second	Very Dissonant
C – E	M3	Major Third	Imperfect Consonance
C – F	P4	Perfect Fourth	Consonance
C – G	P5	Perfect Fifth	Most non-unison Consonance
C – A	M6	Major Sixth	Dynamic Consonance
C – B	M7	Major Seventh	Very Dissonant
C – C	P8	Perfect Octave	Perfect Consonance

The *C* major scale and terms above are just variable ways that you could use the terminology. You could say, "I was playing the fifth of the *C* major scale when you played that *G* chord." Or, "I like to start on the 3rd degree of the *C* major scale when playing over the *E* minor chord."

RECAP:

♫ Steps refer to the distance between notes in a scale, either W or H.

♫ Major scales and their derivatives only use 7 of the 12 notes.

♫ These notes correspond to an interval. The first note is the 1st interval and so on.

♫ These intervals can be categorized into M, m, P, A, & d.

This basis of theory will be developed further as we progress.. I will describe the notation better and its use in the preceding chapters. I will use the interval terminology from here on out. So, if you haven't got it down, look it over once more. Now, we go on to the major scale!

Chapter 5 - *Major Scale Theory in Detail*

The major scale is the foundation of music. If you read the introduction, learning about the major scale is what unlocked music for me. Why is a minor scale, minor? Why is a chord a chord? And many more fascinating questions can be answered by understanding the major scale. This is more true than you know.

A step is a linear, melodic interval between <u>two adjacent notes</u> of a scale.

The major scale is a diatonic scale. This term "diatonic" is used to refer mainly to 8 note scales where 7 of them are of different pitch and 2 are in unison. The word "diatonic" is a Greek word that means literally (*dia*) through – (*tonos*) tones. So, a diatonic scale is a seven toned, eight note scale that passes linearly through successive tones (*A-B-C#-D-E-F#-G#-A* or *C-D-E-F-G-A-B-C*, and many others).

Now we know what a step is, what an interval is, and what diatonic means. Now how do we make this thing? And what use is it to me? There is a formula that we use to make the major scale. This formula is:

Example 5-1:

W – W – H – W – W – W –H   (*NTS:* Know this!!!)

Recall that **W** means **whole step** and **H** means **half step**. Now check this out. We are going to use a keyboard from a piano (Figure 5-1) to help us understand this.

Figure 5-1:

Notice that I only have the naturals *C D E F G A B C* printed on the keyboard. This is because the foundation of music is the major scale, and the foundation of the major scale is the *C major* scale. The step progression illustrated in Example 5-1 is the outline by which we can get the *C major* scale. You can visualize this better if you view each key as a half step. The black keys are the accidentals that lie between certain naturals. Make note that there are 7 naturals and 5 accidentals. It is easier to see this on a piano than on a guitar fretboard.

Root		M2		M3		P4		P5		M6		M7		8va
		W		W		H		W		W		W		H	
C		D		E		F		G		A		B		C

When you go from *C* to *D* it is a whole step, *D* to *E* whole step, *E* to *F* half step, *F* to *G* whole step, *G* to *A* whole step, *A* to *B* whole step, and from *B* back to *C* is a half step. Why isn't the foundation of the major scale *A major* instead of *C major*, and why that step progression?

C major is easy to grasp because it has no sharps or flats. It is usually the first scale that is taught, one of the most used tunings in musical instruments, and highly used as the key that songs are written in. We can learn all of our sharp and flat keys by using the cycle of 5th/4th. *C* major is also a key component to what is referred to as the common practice period.

The common practice period is a time period which includes the Romantic, Baroque, and Classical periods. To get a better understanding of this, looking it up would be a good idea. As a generality though, how we comprise chord progressions with Roman numerals, the modality of music, and counterpoint all derived from out of the common practice period.

TAB 5-1:

TAB 5-1 shows us the *C major* scale played with the root note (the root of *C* major is *C*, duh) on the *A* string, in one octave. The first note and the last note are of the same quality (both are *C*) but the second *C* that is played is of a higher pitch. The term octave (written as *8va*) is Latin for 8. So, it is the 8th note in the scale and is also considered a 1st interval if the scale was to continue in this pattern, and it is of the same note quality as the 1st note. The octave of *C* cannot be *C#*, *D* or any other quality, but only *C*.

Notice that I didn't post a linear TAB of the major scale. That is because that not many people use scales in a linear fashion under most circumstances. It is good knowledge to know this though. The notes are the same enharmonically. That means that the notes are of the same pitch and note quality, but located on a different fret and string. For your rest assurance, I will give you the *C* major scale on one string (linearly).

TAB 5-2:

```
    4                          _____
  # 4                      |  |  |  |
 (  4           ._  ._  ._  ._  |  |  |  |
  1            |   |   |   |   |   |   |   |
              

  T
  A
  B ___3___5___7___8__10_12_14_15_____
```

If you fret out TAB 5-2, you will see that it carries the progression W−W−H−W−W−W−H.

The major scale can be seen as 2 tetrachords separated by a whole tone (W). Each tetrachord is built by two whole steps and a half step. Let me split this up for you, so that you can see it better:

W-W-H   W   W-W-H

And if I write this out by using the notes:

C-D-E-F   *G-A-B-C*

There are different kinds of tetrachords (NTS).

The Major tetrachord: W-W-H

The minor tetrachord: W-H-W

The Phrygian tetrachord: H-W-W

The Gypsy tetrachord: H-WH-H (WH is one and one half steps)

Therefore, two Major tetrachords together makes a major scale.

Figure 5-2 shows the piano notes of the **C** major scale and the two major tetrachords that make it up. Remembering that each key is a half step, we can visually see the whole step, whole step, half step, then there is a whole step separating the two tetrachords and then (starting from **G**) another whole step, whole step, half step.

Figure 5-2:

The major scale is also called the heptatonic scale, meaning that it has 7 different, consecutive notes. The major scale is also considered to have 8 degrees. These degrees correspond to all of the notes in the scale and it includes the octave.

The scale degrees are the numbers that are assigned to the notes in the scale. If we recall there are 8 numbers given to the intervals, as well. These 8 degrees of the major scale have also been given names. The names are so called based on what is referred to as tonality and the key center. The tonic is considered the tonal center.

Here the degrees are listed in order:

Interval	Note	Degree
1st	C	Tonic, key note, root note, root, etc.
2nd	D	Supertonic
3rd	E	Mediant
4th	F	Subdominant
5th	G	Dominant
6th	A	Submediant
7th	B	Leading tone
8th	C	Tonic, octave, 8va

The *supertonic* is a W from the tonic. *Subtonic* would be a W below the tonic. *Mediant*, is a third above the tonic. *Submediant* is a third below the tonic. The median is also in the middle of the tonic and the dominant, whereas the *submediant* is midway between the tonic and the subdominant. The *dominant* is a fifth above the tonic. The *subdominant* is a fifth below the tonic. The *Leading Tone* is a note that leads into the next tone (a semitone higher). That next tone after the leading tone is a resolution, which just means that the dissonance is taken to consonance. There are chords and notes that "feel" like they need to move to the next note. That moving to the next anticipated note is resolution.

This is just another way to vocally identify which degree of the scale that you are referring to. If you are talking about the major scale the mediant would be the 3rd degree of the scale. I usually just say that I "played the 3rd". This would mean that I played the third note of the scale. If I was playing in *C* major it would be the mediant, major 3rd (M3), or more specifically *E*.

Let's put it all together in a table, so that we can see it at one time:

From – To	Degree	Interval	Full Interval Name	Sound
C – C	Tonic	P1	Perfect Unison	Perfect Consonance
C – D	Supertonic	M2	Major Second	Very Dissonant
C – E	Mediant	M3	Major Third	Imperfect Consonance
C – F	Subdominant	P4	Perfect Fourth	Consonance
C – G	Dominant	P5	Perfect Fifth	Most non-unison Consonance
C – A	Submediant	M6	Major Sixth	Dynamic Consonance
C – B	Leading Tone	M7	Major Seventh	Very Dissonant
C – C	Octave	P8	Perfect Octave	Perfect Consonance

Chapter 6 – *Cycle of 5ths and 4ths*

The *C major* scale will be the **ONLY** major scale that is all naturals (***NTS***). All major scales will have at least one # or one *b* in them, except for the *C* major scale. These major scales are also referred to as keys. We will explain why in chord theory, but for now let's use the terminology.

We know how to make a major scale. We know what intervals are in the major scale. We even know the degree names of the major scales, but all we have talked about so far is the *C* major scale. What about the other major scales?

The *C major* scale plays a part in all of the other major scales. We use a method known as the Cycle of 5ths. The Cycle of 5ths is exactly what it sounds like. We take the 5th interval of a major scale and that note becomes the 1st interval of the next major scale.

We first start with the *C* major scale, because it is the foundation of all major scales.

C – D – E – F – G – A – B – C

Then we go to the 5th interval (Remember that *C* is the 1st interval!! Trust me; this is a mistake I see all of the time). This note is *G,* I'll show you:

C – D – E – F – G.

The *G* will now be the 1st interval of the next major scale.

G – A – B – C – D – E – F# – G

Wait a minute… did you remember the step progression?

W–W–H–W–W–W–H

The *C major* scale will be the **ONLY** major scale that is all naturals. I know that I said that before, but I'll say it again. The *C* major scale will be the ONLY *major* scale that is all naturals. This is important for you to understand.

The key of *C major* has produced the next key, *G major*. Let's keep going. We go to the 5th interval of the *G major* scale (notice key and scale are interchangeable when referring to **their** properties, but you play a *G major* scale not a *G major* key. You play *__in__* a *G major* key not a *G major* scale).

G – A – B – C – D

Now the new key is the key of *D major*.

D – E – F♯ – G – A – B – C♯ – D

Go to the 5th interval of *D* major.

D – E – F♯ – G – A

The new key is *A major*.

A – B – C♯ – D – E – F♯ – G♯ – A

This keeps on going until we reach the key of *C♯*, so I'll just put up Figure 5-3 so you can see it as a whole.

Figure 5-3:

C – D – E – F – G – A – B – C

G – A – B – C – D – E – F♯ – G

D – E – F♯ – G – A – B – C♯ – D

A – B – C♯ – D – E – F♯ – G♯ – A

E – F♯ – G♯ – A – B – C♯ – D♯ – E

B – C♯ – D♯ – E – F♯ – G♯ – A♯ – B

F♯ – G♯ – A♯ – B – C♯ – D♯ – E♯ – F♯

C♯ – D♯ – E♯ – F♯ – G♯ – A♯ – B♯ – C♯

You really need to get out a pen and paper and see if you can come up with the same thing that I have. I know you can memorize what I have down already, but I promise that doing it on your own is a great help.

Note that the **C** *maj* scale has no sharps, the **G** *maj* scale has 1 sharp, the **D** *maj* scale has 2 sharps, the **A** *maj* scale has 3 sharps, and so on and so forth. The next thing to note is that **G** *maj* has one sharp and it is the **F#**. **D** *maj* has 2 sharps and they are **F#** and **C#**. **A** *maj* has 3 sharps and they are **F#**, **C#**, and **G#**. Also the new sharp is always the 7th interval. Interesting, isn't it? <u>**NTS:**</u> As the cycle of 5ths progresses, the number of sharps increases.

When you get a sharp, you keep a sharp. This means when you get the **F#** the next key will have the **F#** and another sharp, the **C#**. The next key will be **F#**, **C#**, and another sharp, **G#**. Lastly, know that the new sharp will be the 7th interval. You should be able to see this from studying Figure 5-3. But, if you can't, see Figure 5-4.

Figure 5-4:

Key	No. of #'s	New # added	Total #'s
C – D – E – F – G – A – B – C	0		None
G – A – B – C – D – E – F♯ – G	1	F♯	F♯
D – E – F♯ – G – A – B – C♯ – D	2	C♯	F♯ C♯
A – B – C♯ – D – E – F♯ – G♯ – A	3	G♯	F♯ C♯ G♯
E – F♯ – G♯ – A – B – C♯ – D♯ – E	4	D♯	F♯ C♯ G♯ D♯
B – C♯ – D♯ – E – F♯ – G♯ – A♯ – B	5	A♯	F♯ C♯ G♯ D♯ A♯
F♯ – G♯ – A♯ – B – C♯ – D♯ – E♯ – F♯	6	E♯	F♯ C♯ G♯ D♯ A♯ E♯
C♯ – D♯ – E♯ – F♯ – G♯ – A♯ – B♯ – C♯	7	B♯	F♯ C♯ G♯ D♯ A♯ E♯ B♯

As I have said in the previous chapters, there needs to be one of each alphabetical notes in these scales. That means that the **G** major scale would NOT go **G-A-B-C-D-E-Gb-G**. That is wrong. It's too confusing to talk about a **Gb** and a **G** in the same scale, when you can easily call it an **F#**. If each note has a different letter it keeps from having messy staff notation, as well.

Thus, the key signature on the left hand side of the staff will tell you what key the music is in.

As you can see above, by the treble cleft, there are 3 sharps. The sharps are *F#*, *C#*, and *G#*. How do I know that? For one, the sharps are on the corresponding staff locations for *F*, *C*, and *G*. Also, there is only one major key that has 3 sharps, the *A* major. And as we can see from Figure 5-4, the sharps are *F#*, *C#*, and *G#*.

When the key is indicated on the staff, then all notes printed on the staff are assumed to be in that key, unless they are called out with a flat, sharp, or natural. This cleans up the staff notation a lot. Imagine if we were playing a song in the key of *C#* and notation had all of those sharps all over it. It would be a nightmare to read.

Example 5-2:

The above song passage is in the key of *E*. You can look above at Figure 5-4 and see that E has 4 sharps, but all of the notes in the measures are just notes. No sharped notes. All notes are assumed to fit in that key, and where an *F, C, G,* or *D* note is, you should know that it is an *F#, C#, G#,* or *D#* unless notified otherwise.

I know that I am talking about keys, but the major scale is not just a scale. It is so much more. It will tell you what chords to play, what modes to play, and

which ones not to play. The key is a function of the song and the scale is like a legend to a map. This is in more detail in chord theory (Get my chord theory book).

Tetrachords can be used in the cycle of fifths, as well.

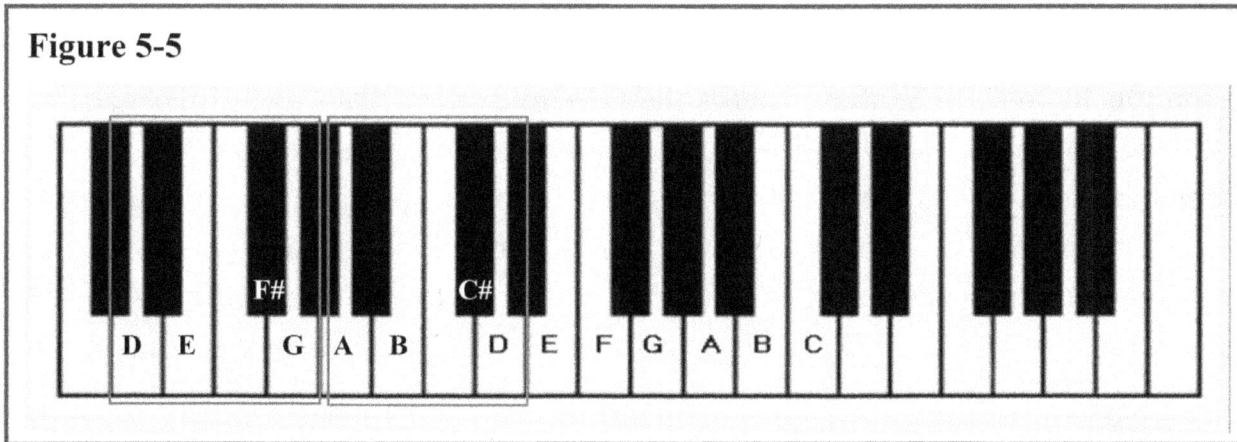

Figure 5-5

In Figure 5-5, up one note from the **C** that we ended on, we start with the **D** and form two tetrachords. This gives us **D-E-F#-G-A-B-C#-D**. If we keep going we can get **E-F#-G#-A-B-C#-D#-E**, and etc. While this eventually gives us all of the major keys, it isn't as useful (in my book, and in my literal book) as the cycle of fifths that I showed you earlier.

I use memorization tools a lot. Let me show you how by using a guitar that we can find the cycle of 5ths.

I will take the first note from each of these major scales (keys) and put them on a fret board.

Figure 5-6:

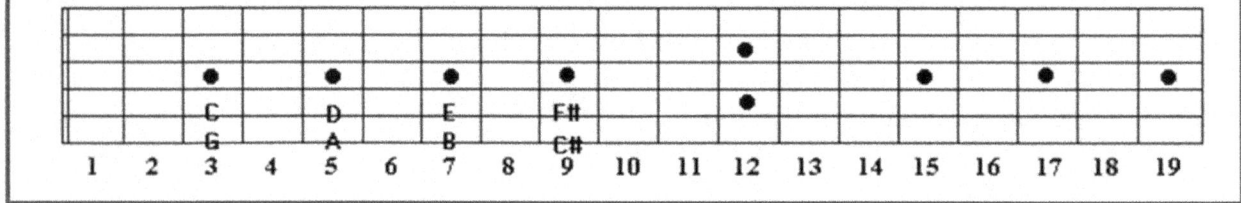

Look at the pattern:

   C is on the 3rd fret. Right above that is the *G*. Move over 2 frets and down a string is the *D*. Then you go up a string to the *A*. And the pattern continues exactly like that until the *C#*. Remember that this is the Cycle of 5ths? Then obviously, a 5th on a guitar is when you move up a string or when you move over 2 frets and down a string. This would be a good thing to remember. There is an exception with the *B* string. You will grow to learn that one string (That tricky little *B* string) usually makes you move over a fret toward the bridge.

   So, in Figure 5-6 these frets are the Cycle of 5ths . When I play this I put my finger on *C* and say, "*C* has no sharps.", then I play the *G* and say, "*G* has one sharp.", and so on and so forth. This is how I memorized them, and if I forgot, it was easy to remember by using that method.

   But wait! There's more! Here is another memory device I use to help remember my sharps added. The first thing to remember is that the newly added sharp is the 7th interval. Most people want to count up to the 7, but it is way easier to move down. Think about it. The 1st interval is also the 8th, then one half step backwards (in a major scale) is the 7th interval. So, what is the sharp in *G*? The *F#*! Which is one half step behind the *G* note. Let me give you an illustration.

Figure 5-7:

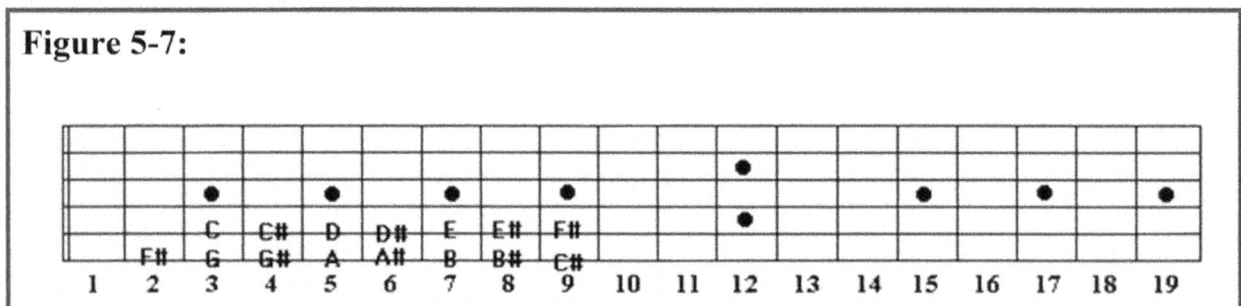

You can easily see by comparing the Figures 5-6 and 5-7 that the new sharps are added much in the same manner that the new sharp keys are added, in 5ths. Let me give you a figure without the sharp keys in it.

Figure 5-8:

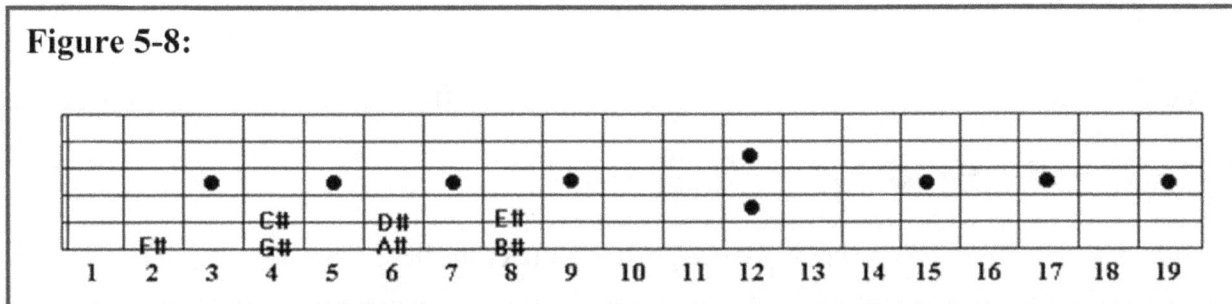

Now you can see the pattern of sharps. For a memory tool, I say *C* has no sharps, *G* has one sharp an *F#*, *D* has two sharps, a *F#* and a *C#*, *A* has three sharps, a *F#*, a *C#*, and a *G#*, and so on. If you go through this method, you can see how this diagram correlates exactly with Figure 5-8.

Again, like Figure 5-6, I practiced this like so: I would put my finger on the *C* and say, "*C* has no sharps", then I would put my finger on the *G* and say, "*G* has one sharp". I would then put my finger on the *F#* and say, "*F#*". I would then play the *D* and say, "*D* has two sharps". Then I would play the *F#* and *C#* and say, "*F#* and *C#*". This is how I made a memorization tool out of it, and like before, if I forgot it wasn't hard to play it and get back on track.

This is very important to know!! Knowing your sharp keys is essential for guitar playing! There are 7 more keys though. These are the flat keys. Guitarists usually don't play in flat keys. These keys are normally used by pianists. If you play with a pianist, you better get to know flat keys. Guitarists hate flat keys and pianists hate sharp keys. Doesn't make sense, but such is life.

So we need to know flat keys. The main ones to store in the memory bank are the keys of *F* and *Bb*. These are the two flat keys that are played most by guitarists. These are the first two flat keys. I will explain all of the keys like before. This time though, we will use the Cycle of 4ths to create the next key (scale).

Again note: The *C major* scale will be the **ONLY** major scale that is all naturals (you should have done a *NTS* on this!!). All major scales will have at least one # or one *b*

---

in them, except for the *C* major scale. These (flat) major scales are also referred to as keys.

The Cycle of 4ths is done exactly like the Cycle of 5ths, but with 4ths. We take the 4th interval of a major scale and that note becomes the 1st interval of the next major scale. Let me show you.

We first start with the C major scale, because it is the foundation of all major scales.

C – D – E – F – G – A – B – C

Then we go to the 4th interval (Remember that *C* is the 1st interval!!). This note is F:

C – D – E – F

The *F* will now be the 1st interval of the next major scale.

F – G – A – Bb – C – D – E – F

The key of *C major* has produced the next key, *F major*. Let's keep going. We go to the 4th interval of the *F major* scale.

F – G – A – Bb

Now the new key is the key of *Bb major*.

Bb – C – D – Eb – F – G – A – Bb

Go to the 4th interval of Bb major.

Bb – C – D – Eb

The new key is *Eb major*.

Eb – F – G – Ab – Bb – C – D – Eb

This keeps on going until we reach the key of *Cb*, so I'll just put up a figure so you can see it as a whole.

Figure 5-9:

$$C - D - E - F - G - A - B - C$$

$$F - G - A - Bb - C - D - E - F$$

$$Bb - C - D - Eb - F - G - A - Bb$$

$$Eb - F - G - Ab - Bb - C - D - Eb$$

$$Ab - Bb - C - Db - Eb - F - G - Ab$$

$$Db - Eb - F - Gb - Ab - Bb - C - Db$$

$$Gb - Ab - Bb - Cb - Db - Eb - F - Gb$$

$$Cb - Db - Eb - Fb - Gb - Ab - Bb - Cb$$

Now, you really need to get out a pen and paper and see if you can come up with the same thing that I have, since I have confused you even more.

Note that the *C maj* scale has no flats, the *F maj* scale has 1 flat, the *Bb maj* scale has 2 flats, the *Eb maj* scale has 3 flats, and so on. The next thing to note is that *F maj* has one flat and it is the *Bb*. *Bb maj* has 2 flats and they are *Bb* and *Eb*. *Eb maj* has 3 flats and they are *Bb*, *Eb*, and *Ab*. Also, the new flat is always the 4th interval. **_NTS:_** As the cycle of 4ths progresses, the number of flats increases. When you get a flat, you keep a flat. Just like with the sharps. This means when you get the *Bb* the next key will have the *Bb*. In fact the next key will be the *Bb* and another flat. The new flat always becomes the next new key. This is much easier to learn than the 5ths. The next key will be *Bb*, *Eb*, and another flat, *Ab*. You should be able to see this from studying Diagram 3-4. But, if you can't, see Figure 5-10.

Figure 5-10:

Key	No. of b's	New b added	Total b's
C – D – E – F – G – A – B – C	0		None
F – G – A – Bb – C – D – E – F	1	Bb	Bb
Bb – C – D – Eb – F – G – A – Bb	2	Eb	Bb Eb
Eb – F – G – Ab – Bb – C – D – Eb	3	Ab	Bb Eb Ab
Ab – Bb – C – Db – Eb – F – G – Ab	4	Db	Bb Eb Ab Db
Db – Eb – F – Gb – Ab – Bb – C – Db	5	Gb	Bb Eb Ab Db Gb
Gb – Ab – Bb – Cb – Db – Eb – F – Gb	6	Cb	Bb Eb Ab Db Gb Cb
Cb – Db – Eb – Fb – Gb – Ab – Bb – Cb	7	Fb	Bb Eb Ab Db Gb Cb

If you take the time to look at both Figure 5-4 and 5-10 beside each other you will see that they are upside down from each other. Here they are in order:

Figure 5-11:

Sharp Key	Flat Key
C – D – E – F – G – A – B – C	C – D – E – F – G – A – B – C
G – A – B – C – D – E – F# – G	F – G – A – Bb – C – D – E – F
D – E – F# – G – A – B – C# – D	Bb – C – D – Eb – F – G – A – Bb
A – B – C# – D – E – F# – G# – A	Eb – F – G – Ab – Bb – C – D – Eb
E – F# – G# – A – B – C# – D# – E	Ab – Bb – C – Db – Eb – F – G – Ab
B – C# – D# – E – F# – G# – A# – B	Db – Eb – F – Gb – Ab – Bb – C – Db
F# – G# – A# – B – C# – D# – E# – F#	Gb – Ab – Bb – Cb – Db – Eb – F – Gb
C# – D# – E# – F# – G# – A# – B# – C#	Cb – Db – Eb – Fb – Gb – Ab – Bb – Cb

Now I will invert (flip) the flat keys upside down.

Sharp Key	Flat Key
C – D – E – F – G – A – B – C	Cb – Db – Eb – Fb – Gb – Ab – Bb – Cb
G – A – B – C – D – E – F# – G	Gb – Ab – Bb – Cb – Db – Eb – F – Gb
D – E – F# – G – A – B – C# – D	Db – Eb – F – Gb – Ab – Bb – C – Db
A – B – C# – D – E – F# – G# – A	Ab – Bb – C – Db – Eb – F – G – Ab
E – F# – G# – A – B – C# – D# – E	Eb – F – G – Ab – Bb – C – D – Eb
B – C# – D# – E – F# – G# – A# – B	Bb – C – D – Eb – F – G – A – Bb
F# – G# – A# – B – C# – D# – E# – F#	F – G – A – Bb – C – D – E – F
C# – D# – E# – F# – G# – A# – B# – C#	C – D – E – F – G – A – B – C

The notes correlate to each other now. Isn't that weird??? Well, you don't need to know that, but it does help you to remember things and put them into perspective.

Remember that when looking at the key signature, you can tell what key it is by how many sharps and flats are in the key.

As a test, What is the key in the staff above this sentence? Sorry, not giving you the answer. You have to find it on your own.

Knowing the major keys (scales) will be very useful in the rest of theory, especially chord theory. Take the time to write out the major scales. Figure out how many sharps or flats are in the major scales. Lock this into memory. Some people use Mnemonics like:

Get **D**ave **A**n **E**xtra **B**ass **F**or **C**hristmas

Fred **B**etter **E**at **A**nother **D**ozen **G**reasy **C**orndogs

This works for some people. It may do you some good to try to come up with ones of your own also.

Think about it… If you know what key someone is playing in, then if you want to solo over that key, you just play the scale that the key is in. Playing the key of *C* major? Play the *C* major scale over it. Playing in the key of *G* major? Play the *G* major scale over it. That should be easy enough to understand. I will get into more detail of soloing in another book (that you should get!). So spend some time learning and memorizing.

ABOUT THE AUTHOR

Bryan DeLauney lives in a small town in Alabama where he resides with his lovely wife, Kristen, and their wily cats. He has a degree in chemistry and works in petroleum distribution. Bryan posts online guitar instructions and ideas on YouTube at
http://www.youtube.com/user/delauney
Enjoy playing guitar and God Bless!!